50 Premium Grocery Store Meals

By: Kelly Johnson

Table of Contents

- Truffle Mac & Cheese with Gruyère
- Organic Rotisserie Chicken with Garlic Herb Butter
- Wagyu Beef & Mushroom Risotto
- Lobster Bisque with Sourdough Bread
- Balsamic Glazed Salmon with Quinoa & Roasted Vegetables
- Filet Mignon with Garlic Mashed Potatoes
- Korean BBQ Bulgogi Beef with Jasmine Rice
- Duck Confit with Wild Rice & Cranberry Sauce
- Shrimp Scampi with Handmade Fettuccine
- Blackened Cajun Chicken with Cheddar Grits
- Miso Glazed Cod with Sesame Spinach
- Spicy Tuna Poke Bowl with Avocado & Mango
- Peking Duck Wraps with Hoisin Sauce
- Mediterranean Lamb Kofta with Hummus & Pita
- French Onion Braised Short Ribs
- Thai Green Curry with Coconut Rice
- Gourmet Truffle & Parmesan Tater Tots
- Smoked Brisket with Bourbon BBQ Sauce
- Seafood Paella with Saffron Rice
- Handmade Lobster Ravioli in Lemon Butter Sauce
- Spaghetti Carbonara with Pancetta & Parmesan
- Braised Oxtail Stew with Red Wine Reduction
- Sushi-Grade Sashimi Platter with Wasabi & Soy Sauce
- Butternut Squash Ravioli with Sage Brown Butter
- Peruvian Lomo Saltado with Garlic Rice
- Harissa-Spiced Moroccan Chicken with Couscous
- Maple Bourbon Glazed Pork Chops
- Spicy Jambalaya with Andouille Sausage & Shrimp
- Argentinian Chimichurri Steak with Roasted Potatoes
- Classic Bouillabaisse Seafood Stew
- Teriyaki Glazed Chicken with Sticky Rice
- Lamb Tagine with Apricots & Almonds
- Mongolian Beef Stir-Fry with Crispy Noodles
- Cajun Blackened Red Snapper with Collard Greens
- Pasta Puttanesca with Kalamata Olives & Capers

- Japanese Tonkatsu with Cabbage Slaw
- Greek Moussaka with Eggplant & Béchamel
- Bison Chili with Fire-Roasted Tomatoes
- Coconut Shrimp with Sweet Chili Dipping Sauce
- Heirloom Tomato & Burrata Salad with Aged Balsamic
- Wild Mushroom & Goat Cheese Tart
- Spanish Chorizo & Manchego Tapas Plate
- Classic Coq au Vin with Red Wine Sauce
- Pulled Pork Sliders with Pickled Slaw
- Beef Stroganoff with Handmade Egg Noodles
- Crispy Duck Breast with Orange Glaze
- Handmade Pierogi with Caramelized Onions
- New Orleans Crawfish Étouffée
- Charred Octopus with Lemon & Olive Oil
- BBQ Jackfruit Tacos with Avocado Crema

Truffle Mac & Cheese with Gruyère

Ingredients:

- 12 oz elbow macaroni
- 2 tbsp butter
- 2 tbsp flour
- 2 cups whole milk
- 1 cup shredded Gruyère cheese
- 1/2 cup shredded white cheddar
- 1 tbsp truffle oil
- Salt & black pepper to taste

Instructions:

1. Cook macaroni according to package instructions.
2. In a saucepan, melt butter, whisk in flour, and cook for 1 minute.
3. Gradually add milk, whisking constantly until thickened.
4. Stir in cheeses, truffle oil, salt, and pepper.
5. Toss with macaroni and serve.

Organic Rotisserie Chicken with Garlic Herb Butter

Ingredients:

- 1 whole organic chicken
- 3 tbsp butter, softened
- 3 cloves garlic, minced
- 1 tbsp fresh thyme
- 1 tbsp fresh rosemary, chopped
- 1 tsp salt
- 1/2 tsp black pepper

Instructions:

1. Preheat oven to 375°F (190°C).
2. Mix butter, garlic, thyme, rosemary, salt, and pepper.
3. Rub mixture under the skin and over the chicken.
4. Roast for 1.5 hours, basting occasionally.

Wagyu Beef & Mushroom Risotto

Ingredients:

- 1 cup Arborio rice
- 4 cups beef broth
- 1/2 lb Wagyu beef, diced
- 1/2 cup white wine
- 1 cup mushrooms, sliced
- 1/2 onion, diced
- 2 tbsp butter
- 1/2 cup grated Parmesan

Instructions:

1. Sauté onions and mushrooms in butter.
2. Add rice and cook for 1 minute.
3. Pour in wine, then gradually add broth, stirring frequently.
4. Cook until creamy, then stir in beef and Parmesan.

Lobster Bisque with Sourdough Bread

Ingredients:

- 2 lobster tails
- 2 tbsp butter
- 1/2 onion, chopped
- 2 cloves garlic, minced
- 1/4 cup tomato paste
- 1/2 cup white wine
- 3 cups seafood stock
- 1/2 cup heavy cream

Instructions:

1. Sauté onion and garlic in butter.
2. Stir in tomato paste, wine, and stock. Simmer for 15 minutes.
3. Add lobster meat and cream, then blend until smooth.
4. Serve with sourdough bread.

Balsamic Glazed Salmon with Quinoa & Roasted Vegetables

Ingredients:

- 2 salmon fillets
- 2 tbsp balsamic vinegar
- 1 tbsp honey
- 1 cup cooked quinoa
- 1 cup roasted vegetables (zucchini, bell peppers, carrots)

Instructions:

1. Mix balsamic and honey, then brush over salmon.
2. Bake at 375°F (190°C) for 12 minutes.
3. Serve over quinoa with roasted vegetables.

Filet Mignon with Garlic Mashed Potatoes

Ingredients:

- 2 filet mignon steaks
- 1 tbsp butter
- 2 cloves garlic, minced
- 2 cups mashed potatoes

Instructions:

1. Sear steaks in butter for 3-4 minutes per side.
2. Add garlic and baste steaks, then rest for 5 minutes.
3. Serve with mashed potatoes.

Korean BBQ Bulgogi Beef with Jasmine Rice

Ingredients:

- 1 lb thinly sliced beef
- 1/4 cup soy sauce
- 1 tbsp sesame oil
- 2 tbsp brown sugar
- 2 cloves garlic, minced
- 1 cup cooked jasmine rice

Instructions:

1. Marinate beef in soy sauce, sesame oil, sugar, and garlic for 30 minutes.
2. Sear beef in a hot pan.
3. Serve over jasmine rice.

Duck Confit with Wild Rice & Cranberry Sauce

Ingredients:

- 2 duck legs
- 1 tsp salt
- 1/2 tsp black pepper
- 1 cup wild rice
- 1/2 cup cranberry sauce

Instructions:

1. Season duck with salt and pepper, then roast at 300°F (150°C) for 2 hours.
2. Cook wild rice according to package instructions.
3. Serve with cranberry sauce.

Shrimp Scampi with Handmade Fettuccine

Ingredients:

- 12 oz fettuccine pasta
- 1/2 lb shrimp, peeled
- 2 tbsp butter
- 3 cloves garlic, minced
- 1/2 cup white wine
- 1/4 cup Parmesan

Instructions:

1. Cook pasta and set aside.
2. Sauté garlic in butter, then add shrimp and cook until pink.
3. Deglaze with wine, then toss with pasta and Parmesan.

Blackened Cajun Chicken with Cheddar Grits

Ingredients:

- 2 chicken breasts
- 1 tbsp Cajun seasoning
- 1 tbsp olive oil
- **For Grits:**
    - 1 cup stone-ground grits
    - 3 cups chicken broth
    - 1 cup shredded cheddar cheese
    - 2 tbsp butter

Instructions:

1. Rub chicken with Cajun seasoning.
2. Heat olive oil in a pan, sear chicken for 4–5 minutes per side until blackened and cooked through.
3. Cook grits in chicken broth until thick, then stir in cheese and butter.
4. Serve chicken over cheddar grits.

Miso Glazed Cod with Sesame Spinach

Ingredients:

- 2 cod fillets
- 2 tbsp white miso paste
- 1 tbsp soy sauce
- 1 tbsp mirin
- 1 tsp honey
- **For Spinach:**
    - 2 cups baby spinach
    - 1 tsp sesame oil
    - 1 tsp sesame seeds

Instructions:

1. Mix miso, soy sauce, mirin, and honey, then brush onto cod.
2. Bake at 375°F (190°C) for 12 minutes.
3. Sauté spinach in sesame oil, then sprinkle with sesame seeds.
4. Serve cod with sesame spinach.

Spicy Tuna Poke Bowl with Avocado & Mango

Ingredients:

- 1/2 lb sushi-grade tuna, cubed
- 1 tbsp soy sauce
- 1 tsp sriracha
- 1 tsp sesame oil
- 1/2 avocado, sliced
- 1/2 cup mango, diced
- 1 cup cooked sushi rice
- 1 tsp sesame seeds

Instructions:

1. Toss tuna with soy sauce, sriracha, and sesame oil.
2. Assemble a bowl with rice, tuna, avocado, and mango.
3. Sprinkle with sesame seeds before serving.

Peking Duck Wraps with Hoisin Sauce

Ingredients:

- 2 duck breasts, skin-on
- 1/4 cup hoisin sauce
- 1 tsp five-spice powder
- 6 Mandarin pancakes (or thin tortillas)
- 1/2 cup sliced cucumber
- 1/2 cup sliced green onions

Instructions:

1. Score duck skin, rub with five-spice powder, and sear skin-side down until crispy.
2. Flip and cook for another 3–4 minutes, then slice thinly.
3. Warm pancakes and spread with hoisin sauce.
4. Fill with duck, cucumber, and green onions.

Mediterranean Lamb Kofta with Hummus & Pita

Ingredients:

- 1 lb ground lamb
- 1 tsp cumin
- 1 tsp coriander
- 1/2 tsp cinnamon
- 1 clove garlic, minced
- 1 tbsp chopped parsley
- **For Serving:**
    - Hummus
    - Pita bread

Instructions:

1. Mix lamb with spices, garlic, and parsley. Shape into oval patties.
2. Grill or pan-sear for 3–4 minutes per side.
3. Serve with hummus and pita.

French Onion Braised Short Ribs

Ingredients:

- 2 lbs beef short ribs
- 2 onions, sliced
- 2 cups beef broth
- 1/2 cup red wine
- 2 tbsp butter
- 1 tsp thyme

Instructions:

1. Sear short ribs in butter until browned, then remove.
2. Sauté onions until caramelized, then add thyme, wine, and broth.
3. Return ribs, cover, and braise at 325°F (165°C) for 2.5 hours.

Thai Green Curry with Coconut Rice

Ingredients:

- 1 lb chicken, sliced
- 2 tbsp green curry paste
- 1 can coconut milk
- 1 cup bell peppers, sliced
- 1 cup jasmine rice
- 1 cup coconut milk (for rice)

Instructions:

1. Cook rice in coconut milk.
2. Sauté curry paste in a pan, then add chicken and bell peppers.
3. Pour in coconut milk and simmer for 15 minutes.
4. Serve over coconut rice.

Gourmet Truffle & Parmesan Tater Tots

Ingredients:

- 2 cups frozen tater tots
- 1 tbsp truffle oil
- 1/4 cup grated Parmesan
- 1 tsp chopped parsley

Instructions:

1. Bake tater tots according to package instructions.
2. Toss with truffle oil, Parmesan, and parsley before serving.

Smoked Brisket with Bourbon BBQ Sauce

Ingredients:

- 2 lbs brisket
- 1 tbsp salt
- 1 tbsp black pepper
- **For Sauce:**
    - 1/2 cup bourbon
    - 1/2 cup ketchup
    - 1/4 cup brown sugar
    - 1 tbsp Worcestershire sauce

Instructions:

1. Rub brisket with salt and pepper, then smoke for 6 hours at 225°F (110°C).
2. Simmer bourbon, ketchup, sugar, and Worcestershire sauce for 10 minutes.
3. Brush sauce over brisket before serving.

Seafood Paella with Saffron Rice

Ingredients:

- 1 cup Arborio or bomba rice
- 2 cups seafood broth
- 1/2 tsp saffron
- 1/2 lb shrimp
- 1/2 lb mussels
- 1/2 lb squid, sliced
- 1/2 cup peas
- 1/2 cup diced tomatoes
- 1/2 tsp smoked paprika

Instructions:

1. Sauté tomatoes, peas, and paprika in a pan.
2. Stir in rice, then pour in broth and saffron.
3. Add seafood on top and cook until rice absorbs the broth.

Handmade Lobster Ravioli in Lemon Butter Sauce

Ingredients:

- **For Ravioli Dough:**
    - 2 cups all-purpose flour
    - 2 eggs
    - 1 tbsp olive oil
- **For Filling:**
    - 1/2 cup lobster meat, chopped
    - 1/4 cup ricotta cheese
    - 1 tbsp Parmesan cheese
    - 1/2 tsp lemon zest
- **For Sauce:**
    - 4 tbsp butter
    - Juice of 1 lemon
    - 1 tbsp chopped parsley

Instructions:

1. Mix flour, eggs, and olive oil into a dough. Knead and let rest for 30 minutes.
2. Mix lobster, ricotta, Parmesan, and lemon zest for the filling.
3. Roll out dough, place filling, and seal into ravioli. Boil for 3 minutes.
4. Melt butter, add lemon juice, and toss with ravioli. Garnish with parsley.

Spaghetti Carbonara with Pancetta & Parmesan

Ingredients:

- 12 oz spaghetti
- 4 oz pancetta, diced
- 2 eggs
- 1/2 cup grated Parmesan
- 1 clove garlic, minced
- Black pepper to taste

Instructions:

1. Cook spaghetti and reserve 1/2 cup pasta water.
2. Sauté pancetta and garlic until crispy.
3. Whisk eggs, Parmesan, and black pepper.
4. Toss hot pasta with pancetta, then add egg mixture, stirring quickly.

Braised Oxtail Stew with Red Wine Reduction

Ingredients:

- 2 lbs oxtail
- 2 tbsp flour
- 1 tbsp olive oil
- 1 onion, chopped
- 2 carrots, chopped
- 3 cloves garlic, minced
- 1 cup red wine
- 3 cups beef broth
- 1 tsp thyme

Instructions:

1. Dredge oxtail in flour and brown in oil.
2. Sauté onion, carrots, and garlic.
3. Deglaze with red wine, then add broth and thyme.
4. Simmer for 3 hours until tender.

Sushi-Grade Sashimi Platter with Wasabi & Soy Sauce

Ingredients:

- 4 oz sushi-grade salmon
- 4 oz sushi-grade tuna
- 4 oz yellowtail
- 1 tbsp wasabi
- 1/4 cup soy sauce
- Pickled ginger for garnish

Instructions:

1. Slice fish into thin sashimi cuts.
2. Arrange on a plate with wasabi and soy sauce.
3. Garnish with pickled ginger.

Butternut Squash Ravioli with Sage Brown Butter

Ingredients:

- **For Filling:**
    - 1 cup roasted butternut squash
    - 1/4 cup ricotta cheese
    - 1 tbsp Parmesan cheese
    - 1/2 tsp nutmeg
- **For Sauce:**
    - 4 tbsp butter
    - 6 sage leaves

Instructions:

1. Mix squash, ricotta, Parmesan, and nutmeg for the filling.
2. Roll out fresh pasta dough, fill, and seal ravioli.
3. Boil ravioli for 3 minutes.
4. Melt butter, add sage, and cook until golden brown. Toss with ravioli.

Peruvian Lomo Saltado with Garlic Rice

Ingredients:

- 1 lb beef sirloin, sliced
- 1 red onion, sliced
- 1 tomato, sliced
- 2 tbsp soy sauce
- 1 tbsp vinegar
- 1/2 tsp cumin
- 2 cloves garlic, minced
- 1 cup cooked rice

Instructions:

1. Sauté beef in oil until browned.
2. Add onion, tomato, garlic, soy sauce, vinegar, and cumin. Stir-fry for 3 minutes.
3. Serve over garlic rice.

Harissa-Spiced Moroccan Chicken with Couscous

Ingredients:

- 2 chicken thighs
- 1 tbsp harissa paste
- 1 tsp cumin
- 1/2 tsp paprika
- 1 cup cooked couscous
- 1/4 cup chopped parsley

Instructions:

1. Rub chicken with harissa, cumin, and paprika.
2. Sear in a pan, then bake at 375°F (190°C) for 25 minutes.
3. Serve over couscous, garnished with parsley.

Maple Bourbon Glazed Pork Chops

Ingredients:

- 2 bone-in pork chops
- 1/4 cup maple syrup
- 2 tbsp bourbon
- 1 tbsp Dijon mustard
- 1 tsp soy sauce

Instructions:

1. Sear pork chops in a pan.
2. Mix maple syrup, bourbon, mustard, and soy sauce.
3. Glaze pork chops, then bake at 375°F (190°C) for 10 minutes.

Spicy Jambalaya with Andouille Sausage & Shrimp

Ingredients:

- 1/2 lb andouille sausage, sliced
- 1/2 lb shrimp
- 1 cup rice
- 2 cups chicken broth
- 1 can diced tomatoes
- 1/2 green bell pepper, chopped
- 1/2 onion, chopped
- 1 tsp Cajun seasoning

Instructions:

1. Sauté sausage, onion, and bell pepper.
2. Stir in rice, tomatoes, broth, and Cajun seasoning.
3. Simmer for 20 minutes, then add shrimp and cook for 5 minutes.

Argentinian Chimichurri Steak with Roasted Potatoes

Ingredients:

- 1 lb flank steak
- **For Chimichurri Sauce:**
    - 1/2 cup parsley, chopped
    - 2 cloves garlic, minced
    - 1/4 cup olive oil
    - 1 tbsp red wine vinegar
    - 1/2 tsp red pepper flakes
- **For Potatoes:**
    - 2 cups baby potatoes, halved
    - 1 tbsp olive oil
    - 1/2 tsp salt

Instructions:

1. Roast potatoes at 400°F (200°C) for 25 minutes.
2. Grill steak to preferred doneness, then rest.
3. Mix chimichurri ingredients and drizzle over steak.
4. Serve with roasted potatoes.

Classic Bouillabaisse Seafood Stew

Ingredients:

- 1/2 lb white fish (cod, halibut), cut into chunks
- 1/2 lb mussels or clams, cleaned
- 1/2 lb shrimp, peeled
- 2 tbsp olive oil
- 1 onion, diced
- 2 cloves garlic, minced
- 1 fennel bulb, sliced
- 1/2 tsp saffron
- 1/2 tsp thyme
- 1 can (14.5 oz) diced tomatoes
- 3 cups seafood broth
- 1/2 cup white wine
- Salt & pepper to taste

Instructions:

1. Sauté onion, garlic, and fennel in olive oil.
2. Add saffron, thyme, tomatoes, wine, and broth. Simmer for 15 minutes.
3. Add fish, mussels, and shrimp. Cook until seafood is done.
4. Serve with crusty bread.

Teriyaki Glazed Chicken with Sticky Rice

Ingredients:

- 2 boneless chicken thighs
- 1/4 cup soy sauce
- 2 tbsp honey
- 1 tbsp mirin
- 1 tsp sesame oil
- 1 clove garlic, minced
- 1 tsp ginger, grated
- 1 cup sushi rice

Instructions:

1. Cook rice and set aside.
2. Mix soy sauce, honey, mirin, sesame oil, garlic, and ginger.
3. Marinate chicken for 30 minutes, then sear in a pan until cooked.
4. Reduce marinade into a glaze and pour over chicken.
5. Serve with sticky rice.

Lamb Tagine with Apricots & Almonds

Ingredients:

- 1 lb lamb shoulder, cubed
- 1 onion, chopped
- 2 cloves garlic, minced
- 1 tsp cinnamon
- 1/2 tsp cumin
- 1/2 tsp paprika
- 1/2 cup dried apricots, chopped
- 1/4 cup almonds
- 2 cups beef broth

Instructions:

1. Sear lamb in a tagine or Dutch oven.
2. Add onion, garlic, and spices, then sauté for 5 minutes.
3. Add apricots, almonds, and broth. Simmer for 1.5 hours until tender.

Mongolian Beef Stir-Fry with Crispy Noodles

Ingredients:

- 1 lb flank steak, sliced
- 2 tbsp cornstarch
- 1/4 cup soy sauce
- 2 tbsp brown sugar
- 1 tsp ginger, grated
- 1 clove garlic, minced
- 1/2 cup green onions, sliced
- 1 cup crispy fried noodles

Instructions:

1. Toss beef with cornstarch and let sit for 10 minutes.
2. Sear in a hot pan until crispy.
3. Stir in soy sauce, brown sugar, ginger, and garlic. Cook for 2 minutes.
4. Serve over crispy noodles, garnished with green onions.

Cajun Blackened Red Snapper with Collard Greens

Ingredients:

- 2 red snapper fillets
- 1 tbsp Cajun seasoning
- 1 tbsp butter
- **For Collard Greens:**
    - 2 cups collard greens, chopped
    - 2 cloves garlic, minced
    - 1/2 cup chicken broth

Instructions:

1. Rub fish with Cajun seasoning.
2. Sear in butter for 3 minutes per side until blackened.
3. Sauté garlic and collard greens, then add broth and simmer for 10 minutes.
4. Serve fish over collard greens.

Pasta Puttanesca with Kalamata Olives & Capers

Ingredients:

- 12 oz spaghetti
- 2 tbsp olive oil
- 3 cloves garlic, minced
- 1/2 tsp red pepper flakes
- 1 can (14.5 oz) diced tomatoes
- 1/4 cup Kalamata olives, sliced
- 2 tbsp capers
- 1 tsp oregano

Instructions:

1. Cook spaghetti and set aside.
2. Sauté garlic and red pepper flakes in olive oil.
3. Add tomatoes, olives, capers, and oregano. Simmer for 10 minutes.
4. Toss with spaghetti and serve.

Japanese Tonkatsu with Cabbage Slaw

Ingredients:

- 2 boneless pork chops
- 1/2 cup panko breadcrumbs
- 1/4 cup flour
- 1 egg, beaten
- **For Slaw:**
    - 1 cup shredded cabbage
    - 1 tbsp rice vinegar
    - 1 tsp sesame oil

Instructions:

1. Dredge pork chops in flour, egg, then panko.
2. Fry in oil at 350°F (175°C) until golden.
3. Mix cabbage with rice vinegar and sesame oil for slaw.
4. Serve tonkatsu with slaw and tonkatsu sauce.

Greek Moussaka with Eggplant & Béchamel

Ingredients:

- 1 lb ground lamb or beef
- 1 onion, chopped
- 2 cloves garlic, minced
- 1/2 tsp cinnamon
- 1 can (14.5 oz) diced tomatoes
- 1 eggplant, sliced
- **For Béchamel:**
    - 2 tbsp butter
    - 2 tbsp flour
    - 1 cup milk
    - 1/2 cup grated Parmesan

Instructions:

1. Sauté onion, garlic, and meat. Add cinnamon and tomatoes, then simmer.
2. Roast eggplant slices at 375°F (190°C) for 15 minutes.
3. Make béchamel by whisking butter, flour, and milk until thick.
4. Layer eggplant, meat sauce, and béchamel in a dish. Bake at 375°F (190°C) for 30 minutes.

Bison Chili with Fire-Roasted Tomatoes

Ingredients:

- 1 lb ground bison
- 1 onion, chopped
- 3 cloves garlic, minced
- 1 can (14.5 oz) fire-roasted tomatoes
- 1 can (15 oz) kidney beans, drained
- 2 cups beef broth
- 1 tbsp chili powder
- 1/2 tsp cumin

Instructions:

1. Sauté onion and garlic, then brown bison.
2. Stir in tomatoes, beans, broth, and spices.
3. Simmer for 45 minutes before serving.

Coconut Shrimp with Sweet Chili Dipping Sauce

Ingredients:

- 1/2 lb large shrimp, peeled & deveined
- 1/2 cup flour
- 2 eggs, beaten
- 1 cup shredded coconut
- 1/2 cup panko breadcrumbs
- 1/2 tsp salt
- Oil for frying
- **For Sauce:**
    - 1/2 cup sweet chili sauce
    - 1 tbsp lime juice

Instructions:

1. Dredge shrimp in flour, dip in egg, then coat in a mixture of coconut, panko, and salt.
2. Heat oil to 350°F (175°C) and fry shrimp until golden brown.
3. Mix sweet chili sauce with lime juice and serve with shrimp.

Heirloom Tomato & Burrata Salad with Aged Balsamic

Ingredients:

- 2 heirloom tomatoes, sliced
- 1 ball burrata cheese
- 2 tbsp olive oil
- 1 tbsp aged balsamic vinegar
- Fresh basil leaves
- Salt & black pepper to taste

Instructions:

1. Arrange tomato slices on a plate.
2. Tear burrata into pieces and place on top.
3. Drizzle with olive oil and balsamic.
4. Garnish with basil and season with salt and pepper.

Wild Mushroom & Goat Cheese Tart

Ingredients:

- 1 sheet puff pastry, thawed
- 1 cup mixed wild mushrooms, sliced
- 1/2 cup goat cheese, crumbled
- 1/4 cup heavy cream
- 1 egg
- 1 tbsp olive oil
- 1/2 tsp thyme

Instructions:

1. Preheat oven to 375°F (190°C).
2. Sauté mushrooms in olive oil with thyme.
3. Mix egg and heavy cream, then stir in goat cheese.
4. Spread mixture onto puff pastry, top with mushrooms, and bake for 20 minutes.

Spanish Chorizo & Manchego Tapas Plate

Ingredients:

- 4 oz Spanish chorizo, sliced
- 4 oz Manchego cheese, sliced
- 1/4 cup Marcona almonds
- 1/4 cup olives
- 1 tbsp honey

Instructions:

1. Arrange chorizo and Manchego on a serving board.
2. Add almonds, olives, and drizzle honey over the cheese.

Classic Coq au Vin with Red Wine Sauce

Ingredients:

- 4 bone-in chicken thighs
- 1 cup red wine
- 1 cup chicken broth
- 1/2 onion, chopped
- 2 cloves garlic, minced
- 1/2 cup mushrooms, sliced
- 1/4 cup pancetta, diced
- 1 tbsp butter
- 1/2 tsp thyme

Instructions:

1. Sear chicken in butter, then remove.
2. Sauté pancetta, onion, garlic, and mushrooms.
3. Add wine, broth, and thyme, then return chicken.
4. Simmer for 45 minutes until chicken is tender.

Pulled Pork Sliders with Pickled Slaw

Ingredients:

- 1 lb pork shoulder
- 1 cup BBQ sauce
- 1 tsp smoked paprika
- 1/2 tsp salt
- **For Slaw:**
    - 1/2 cup shredded cabbage
    - 2 tbsp apple cider vinegar
    - 1/2 tsp sugar
    - 1/2 tsp salt
- 6 slider buns

Instructions:

1. Slow-cook pork with paprika and salt at 300°F (150°C) for 4 hours. Shred and mix with BBQ sauce.
2. Toss cabbage with vinegar, sugar, and salt.
3. Serve pork on buns with pickled slaw.

Beef Stroganoff with Handmade Egg Noodles

Ingredients:

- **For Noodles:**
    - 2 cups flour
    - 2 eggs
    - 1 tbsp olive oil
- **For Stroganoff:**
    - 1 lb beef sirloin, sliced
    - 1/2 cup mushrooms, sliced
    - 1/2 cup sour cream
    - 1/2 cup beef broth
    - 1/4 cup onion, chopped
    - 1 tbsp butter

Instructions:

1. Mix flour, eggs, and oil to form pasta dough. Roll out and cut into noodles.
2. Boil noodles for 3 minutes.
3. Sear beef in butter, then remove.
4. Sauté onion and mushrooms, add broth, then stir in sour cream and beef.
5. Serve over egg noodles.

Crispy Duck Breast with Orange Glaze

Ingredients:

- 2 duck breasts, skin-on
- 1/2 tsp salt
- 1/4 tsp black pepper
- **For Orange Glaze:**
    - 1/2 cup fresh orange juice
    - 1 tbsp honey
    - 1 tbsp balsamic vinegar
    - 1 tsp Dijon mustard

Instructions:

1. Score duck skin in a crisscross pattern. Season with salt and pepper.
2. Place duck skin-side down in a cold pan and cook over medium heat for 6–8 minutes until crispy. Flip and cook for another 3–4 minutes.
3. Remove duck and let rest.
4. In the same pan, add orange juice, honey, balsamic vinegar, and mustard. Simmer until thickened.
5. Slice duck and drizzle with orange glaze.

Handmade Pierogi with Caramelized Onions

Ingredients:

- **For Dough:**
    - 2 cups flour
    - 1/2 tsp salt
    - 1/2 cup sour cream
    - 1 egg
    - 2 tbsp butter, melted
- **For Filling:**
    - 1 cup mashed potatoes
    - 1/2 cup shredded cheddar cheese
    - Salt & pepper to taste
- **For Topping:**
    - 1 onion, thinly sliced
    - 2 tbsp butter

Instructions:

1. Mix dough ingredients, knead, and let rest for 30 minutes.
2. Mix mashed potatoes with cheese, salt, and pepper.
3. Roll out dough and cut into circles. Fill with potato mixture and seal.
4. Boil pierogi until they float, then pan-fry in butter.
5. Sauté onions in butter until caramelized, then serve over pierogi.

New Orleans Crawfish Étouffée

Ingredients:

- 1/2 lb crawfish tails
- 2 tbsp butter
- 1/4 cup flour
- 1/2 onion, chopped
- 1/2 green bell pepper, chopped
- 2 cloves garlic, minced
- 2 cups seafood broth
- 1 tsp Cajun seasoning
- 1/2 tsp paprika
- 1/2 tsp thyme
- 1/4 cup green onions, sliced

Instructions:

1. Make a roux by cooking butter and flour until golden brown.
2. Add onion, bell pepper, and garlic. Cook until soft.
3. Stir in broth, Cajun seasoning, paprika, and thyme. Simmer for 10 minutes.
4. Add crawfish and cook for 5 minutes.
5. Serve over rice, garnished with green onions.

Charred Octopus with Lemon & Olive Oil

Ingredients:

- 1 whole octopus (about 1 lb)
- 1 lemon, juiced
- 2 tbsp olive oil
- 2 cloves garlic, minced
- 1/2 tsp smoked paprika
- 1/4 tsp salt
- 1/4 tsp black pepper

Instructions:

1. Simmer octopus in salted water for 45 minutes until tender.
2. Remove and let cool, then slice into pieces.
3. Toss with olive oil, garlic, paprika, salt, and pepper.
4. Grill or sear in a hot pan for 3–4 minutes until charred.
5. Drizzle with lemon juice before serving.

BBQ Jackfruit Tacos with Avocado Crema

Ingredients:

- 1 can (14 oz) young jackfruit, drained and shredded
- 1/2 cup BBQ sauce
- 1/2 tsp smoked paprika
- 1/2 tsp cumin
- **For Avocado Crema:**
    - 1 ripe avocado
    - 1/4 cup sour cream or yogurt
    - 1 tbsp lime juice
    - 1/2 tsp garlic powder
- **For Serving:**
    - 6 small corn tortillas
    - 1/4 cup chopped cilantro
    - 1/4 cup sliced red onion

Instructions:

1. Sauté jackfruit with smoked paprika and cumin for 5 minutes.
2. Stir in BBQ sauce and cook for another 5 minutes.
3. Blend avocado, sour cream, lime juice, and garlic powder for crema.
4. Warm tortillas and fill with jackfruit.
5. Top with avocado crema, cilantro, and red onion.

www.ingramcontent.com/pod-product-compliance
Lightning Source LLC
LaVergne TN
LVHW081500060526
838201LV00056BA/2846